For Ursula, with love – K.F.

To A, your constant support is what keeps me going – A.C.

First published in Great Britain 2025 by Red Shed, part of Farshore
An imprint of HarperCollins*Publishers*
1 London Bridge Street, London SE1 9GF
www.farshore.co.uk

HarperCollins*Publishers*
Macken House, 39/40 Mayor Street Upper,
Dublin 1, D01 C9W8, Ireland

Red Shed is a registered trademark of HarperCollins*Publishers* Ltd.

Text © HarperCollins*Publishers* 2025
Illustrations © Aaron Cushley 2025
Aaron Cushley has asserted his moral rights.

Consultancy by Dr Steven Ashby, Dr Kamal Badreshany, Professor Paul Barrett, Professor Emeritus Colin Divall, Dr Caroline Dodds Pennock, Professor Rebecca Earle, Dr Lisa McGerty, Dr Joanna Piotrowska and Professor Martin Polley.

ISBN 978 0 00 856815 3
Printed and bound in Malaysia
001

A CIP catalogue record for this title is available from the British Library.

All rights reserved. No part of this publication may be reproduced, stored in a retrieval system, or transmitted, in any form or by any means, electronic, mechanical, photocopying, recording or otherwise, without the prior permission of the publisher and copyright owner.

Without limiting the author's and publisher's exclusive rights, any unauthorised use of this publication to train generative artificial intelligence (AI) technologies is expressly prohibited. HarperCollins also exercise their rights under Article 4(3) of the Digital Single Market Directive 2019/790 and expressly reserve this publication from the text and data mining exception.

Stay safe online. Any website addresses listed in this book are correct at the time of going to print. However, Farshore is not responsible for content hosted by third parties. Please be aware that online content can be subject to change and websites can contain content that is unsuitable for children. We advise that all children are supervised when using the internet.

This book contains FSC™ certified paper and other controlled sources to ensure responsible forest management.

For more information visit: www.harpercollins.co.uk/green

WHAT CAME FIRST?

Kit Frost & Aaron Cushley

INTRODUCTION

What do YOU love to find out about? Science? Sport? Animals? Is it the incredible prehistoric world of the dinosaurs, or the ancient Egyptians with their epic pyramids? Astronauts soaring into space, or computers and video games?

In this book you'll find all of these and more . . . but instead of zooming IN to find out about just one thing at a time, we'll be zooming OUT and looking at the world as one enormous timeline of EVERYTHING. Along the way, you'll find the surprising answers to all sorts of questions – such as . . .

Is the enormous Mount Everest older than sharks?

What's the oldest pair of socks? (Hold your nose!)

Did Saturn's rings form before dinosaurs walked the Earth?

Get ready to hurtle around the world and back in time, and get your fact-finding brain whirring. Your task is simple . . .

- Find the questions on each page.
- Guess what came first for each one.
- Once you've had a go, read on to see if you guessed correctly.
- Use the mind-boggling facts you've found to impress your teachers, family and friends!

Let's get started with a classic 'what came first' question.

THE CHICKEN OR THE EGG?

Chickens hatch from eggs, but eggs are laid by chickens . . . it's a puzzle, but we can solve it once and for all.

The egg came first! Over time, all birds gradually evolved from ancient reptiles. The first bird hatched from an egg that was laid by a reptile with some bird characteristics. Birds have been evolving and changing for millions of years – modern chickens are descended from a wild bird called the red junglefowl.

Chickens and ostriches are actually Tyrannosaurus' closest relatives alive today!

READY FOR MORE? TURN THE PAGE TO GET STARTED!

THEME PARKS OR SKATEPARKS?

If you guessed theme parks, nice work – you're absolutely right! Strap in and get ready for a rollercoaster ride through time . . .

Theme parks

If you like a dose of adventure, theme parks are the perfect choice. The world's oldest theme park opened in Denmark way back in 1583. It is called Bakken, and it is still open today. There are lots of rides for visitors to enjoy, including a wooden rollercoaster that has been there since 1932. So much of the rollercoaster has been repaired and replaced though, that there's not much of the original track left!

Skateparks

Like lots of skaters today, early skaters practised on any downhill slope they could find. The world's first skatepark opened in Albany, Oregon, in July 1965 – it was a simple wooden track with curves and slopes. Today, there are thousands of skateparks around the world with exciting ramps and obstacles. Skateboarding also became an Olympic sport in 2020.

It's thought that skateboarding was invented in the late 1950s by surfers in California. They were looking for ways of surfing when the sea was calm and flat!

CHESS OR DRAUGHTS?

Draughts beats chess by a long way. It had been popular for around 2,000 years before chess was invented!

Draughts
A Middle Eastern game called alquerque, dating from 1400BCE, was an early ancestor of the game. The name and rules of draughts have varied over time, so it's tricky to put an exact date on when it was invented!

Chess
An early version of chess, called chaturanga, was played in India from around 600CE. It caught on and spread around the world as people travelled and traded.

A game for a queen
The Egyptian pharaoh Hatshepsut may have been a draughts fan. When she died around 1458BCE, a board was placed in her tomb. Perhaps she was looking forward to a game in the afterlife?

ROCK, PAPER, SCISSORS OR THUMB WAR?

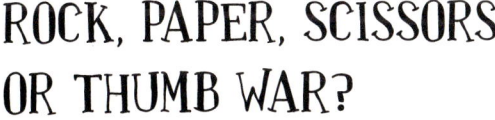

Rock, paper, scissors! This game originated in China around 200BCE, though the objects used have changed over time. Cloth is sometimes used instead of paper, and an early version had a frog, a slug and a snake! The origins of thumb wars are unclear – some people claim it was created in the USA around 1930–1940.

YO-YOS OR MARBLES?

Marbles! Some examples have been found that date back to around 2500BCE. These original ones were made of stone, often marble (giving them their name). The first written record of the yo-yo was in ancient Greece, between 500–400BCE.

TYRANNOSAURUS OR STEGOSAURUS?

Give a big dinosaur drumroll... Stegosaurus came first, by a long way; 80 million years, to be exact!

Stegosaurus

This spiny dinosaur lived between around 155–150 million years ago, during the Late Jurassic period. Though Stegosaurus was around nine metres long, its brain was just the size of a lemon!

Keep away!
Stegosaurus used its spiky tail to defend itself from predators.

Huge heads
Tyrannosaurus' head was about 1.5 metres long. How tall is that compared to you? Ask an adult to help you measure.

Tyrannosaurus

The ferocious Tyrannosaurus, with teeth larger than the height of this book, stomped in during the Late Cretaceous period – around 80 million years AFTER Stegosaurus had become extinct. So, Stegosaurus would never even have met Tyrannosaurus!

A shared home

Though these two dinosaurs were very far apart in time, they both lived in the part of the world we now call North America.

If you put Tyrannosaurus, Stegosaurus and the first humans on a timeline, Tyrannosaurus would be closer to humans than to Stegosaurus!

BLUE WHALES OR WOOLLY MAMMOTHS?

The long-extinct woolly mammoth might seem older than the blue whale – but it was the whale that came first!

Blue whales

These impressive animals are the biggest that have EVER lived – and they are still swimming in our oceans. They first appeared looking as they do today around 1.5 million years ago. They would have been able to splash their tails at *Homo habilis*, an early human, but would have had to wait a long time to splash them at a woolly mammoth!

Woolly mammoths

As you might have guessed, woolly mammoths are related to elephants. Elephant ancestors have been around for millions of years, but woolly mammoths only evolved as their own species around 0.8 million years ago. They became extinct around 4,000 years ago.

*An early ancestor of whales, called **Pakicetus**, lived around 50 million years ago. It was a land animal with four legs!*

THE CAN OR THE CAN OPENER?

You might think that the can opener was invented at the same time as the can . . . but you'd be wrong! The can opener was actually invented a whopping 48 years AFTER the can. Let's see how it all started . . .

Early cans were made of thick metal. You needed a hammer and a chisel to open them – hardly an easy meal!

1809: Bottling invented

Before anyone even thought of cans, Frenchman Nicholas Appert worked out that food could be kept fresh by putting it in a sealed bottle that was then heated up.

1810: First cans

Englishman Peter Durand received a patent for preserving food in cans.

Super certificates
A patent is a document that inventors are given to say something was their idea.

1858: First can opener

At last, American Ezra J. Warner invented the first can opener. However, it was hard to use, and left sharp, jagged edges from sawing around the can. Ouch! Many people in the mid-1800s would ask their local shop to open cans for them.

1920s: Modernised design

Over 100 years after Nicholas Appert's bottling success, a can opener with a wheel, like the type we still use today, was invented. Finally!

FLUSHING TOILETS OR TOILET PAPER?

Flushing toilets might seem like a shiny, new invention next to the humble loo roll – but they are actually MUCH older!

Flushing toilets

Picture yourself on the ancient Greek island of Crete. Sun, a gentle breeze, the sound of running water – but it's not the sea . . . it's the home of what's thought to be one of the world's oldest flushing toilets! It was built by the Minoans (an early Greek civilisation) around 3,500 years ago. No toilet paper, though – they probably made do with pebbles or small pieces of pottery. That can't have been comfortable!

Over history, people have used all sorts of things to wipe themselves with after going to the toilet – including dried-up corncobs in North and South America.

Toilet paper

Paper was invented in China around 105CE, about 1,500 years after the Minoan toilet – but paper made just to use on the toilet came later. The first toilet paper was created in 1391, for the Chinese emperor and his family. It was perfumed!

Before 1391, people did sometimes use their writing paper on the loo. In 589CE, Chinese scholar Yen Chih-Thui wrote that there were some pieces of writing he wouldn't dare use as toilet paper. He didn't want to wipe his bottom with the names of wise writers!

Roll up, roll up!
Toilet paper rolls, as you might recognise them today, were officially patented in the USA in 1857.

COMPUTERS OR TELEPHONES?

Did you guess the telephone? If you did, you're right in one way because the first telephones were used before the first computers. But computers were actually invented first!

Computers

So, what caused the delay for computers? Well, money was the main reason. English mathematician Charles Babbage worked on two computers from the 1820s–1850s, but they were so large and complicated that funding kept running out! Sadly, none of Babbage's machines were built during his lifetime.

Technology moves on

Fast forward to the 1940s – electronic, digital, programmable computers were created. The first, called Colossus, was used for codebreaking in England during World War II.

Programming pioneer
Ada Lovelace, another mathematician who lived in the 1800s, created the first computer programme, designed for Charles Babbage's machine.

Telephones

The telephone was created by Scottish-born American inventor Alexander Graham Bell. He made the first phone call on 10 March 1876, over 50 years after Babbage's first computer design. He called up his assistant who was in a room nearby, saying, "Mr Watson – come here – I want to see you."

Ring, ring!

In the USA in 1876, there were around 3,000 telephones. In 1900, this number was more than 100 times higher, at around 356,000 telephones!

TOUCHSCREENS OR EMOJIS?

Did you give a thumbs-up to emojis? They were created around 30 years ago . . . but touchscreens have been around for over 50 years!

Touchscreens

Nowadays, swiping and tapping on touchscreens feels like second nature. But did you know that they were first invented in 1965 by British engineer Eric Johnson to help with air traffic control systems? The first phone with a touchscreen, the IBM Simon, launched in 1994.

Emojis

Sometimes, the best message is a smiley face emoji (or a smiley poo!). The first set of these symbols, used in text messages instead of words, was made in 1999 by Japanese designer Shigetaka Kurita.

VIDEO GAMES OR DIGITAL CAMERAS?

It's true that cameras have been around since the 1800s, but the first digital camera is younger than video games!

The first arcade computer game, developed in 1971, was called Computer Space – but it wasn't a big success. Video games started to take off later in the 1970s, with games such as Pong and Space Invaders.

Video games

Early computer games were used to show how machines worked, but in 1958, American physicist William Higinbotham created a game made as something fun to play! It was called *Tennis for Two*.

Digital cameras

We have American inventor Steve Sasson to thank for our digital snaps. He created the first portable digital camera in 1975 – though it wasn't all that portable. It was about the size of a toaster!

PANTS OR SOCKS?

Pants are probably older — though we don't know for sure, because the natural skins and fabrics that were used to make ancient pants and socks usually rotted quickly.

Pants
It's likely that prehistoric humans wore loincloths (simple underwear) made of animal skins. The oldest known loincloth was found on a 5,300-year-old person preserved in ice. But perhaps older ones no longer exist or have not yet been found?

Socks
The oldest known pair of socks is from the ancient Egyptian city of Oxyrhynchus. They are around 1,700 years old, are a jaunty red colour, and have two toes. This means that they were probably designed to wear with sandals!

BRISTLED TOOTHBRUSHES OR TOOTHPASTE?

Have you been brushing up on your history? If you said toothpaste, you're spot on!

Twigs have been used as a kind of brush for at least 5,500 years. Chewing the end of a twig can create a form of brush from the frayed end.

Toothpaste
Ancient Egyptians, Greeks and Romans all made their own toothpaste. One ancient Egyptian recipe from around 1,600 years ago includes salt, pepper, mint, iris flowers and ground-up rocks. The ancient Greeks used ground-up shells and bones. These rough materials helped rub away dirt in a similar way to your toothpaste today — but yours is much gentler!

Toothbrushes
Bristled toothbrushes, similar to the ones we use today, were invented in China over 1,000 years ago. These early brushes had bamboo handles and bristles made from pigs' hair.

ELECTRIC FRIDGES OR MICROWAVE OVENS?

Fridges! The first electric refrigerator for use at home was invented in 1913, by American engineer Fred W. Wolf. Microwave ovens were invented 32 years later in 1945 – they were expensive at first, and only became widely used in the 1970s.

Electric fridges

Before fridges, wealthy people would store big blocks of ice in ice houses, usually with an underground chamber to keep the ice frozen for as long as possible. Blocks would be transferred to smaller ice boxes in the home, used to keep food cool and preserve it. Fred W. Wolf's fridge included an ice box!

A microwave is a type of radiation (a transfer of energy). Inside a microwave oven, the microwaves transfer energy to the water molecules in food. This heats the food, ready to eat!

Microwave ovens

An American scientist named Percy Spencer figured out that microwaves could be used on food. He was experimenting with a magnetron (a piece of equipment that produces microwaves). During one experiment, he noticed a sugary peanut snack bar in his pocket had melted! His discovery led to the invention of the microwave oven – a device that millions use every day.

PLANES OR HELICOPTERS?

When it comes to the planes and helicopters you'd recognise today, planes came first! Let's zoom into the clouds and take a look at these amazing flying machines . . .

Planes

Around 120 years ago in 1903, brothers Wilbur and Orville Wright took off on the first successful engine-powered plane flight, in North Carolina, USA. They travelled 36 metres – the length of around seven giraffes lying end to end!

Helicopters

These vehicles with their spinning rotors weren't far behind. In 1907, French engineer Paul Cornu developed a helicopter that could carry a person – though only 1.5 metres off the ground . . . Many other inventors worked on similar machines, and by the 1930s there were helicopters that could reach heights of over 3,000 metres.

A glider
This design had bat-like wings.

An aerial screw
This had a rotor a bit like a helicopter's.

Imagination flying high

People dreamed of flying for a long time before they actually did! Around 500 years ago, Italian artist and inventor Leonardo da Vinci designed human-powered flying machines like the illustrations to the left and right – though his incredible designs were never actually built.

WHEELS OR BOATS?

Boats came first – though they both deserve a special mention for being REALLY old.

Boats

The oldest boat ever discovered is a Dutch canoe that is a whopping 10,000 years old, but humans were using boats even earlier to move around. The wood and other natural materials used to make boats rot easily though, so remains are rare.

Wheels

It's not clear exactly when the wheel was invented. Some examples are around 5,000–6,000 years old, including a collection of drinking cups from 3900BCE found in eastern Europe – each had a set of wheels! The reason why is still a mystery. What's your guess?

UNDERGROUND TRAINS OR SUBMARINES?

Submarines might seem modern, but they've been around for longer than underground trains. Take a deep breath and let's head underwater and underground . . .

Submarines

The first successful dive from an underwater vessel happened in the River Thames, in London, around 400 years ago in 1620. It was created by Dutch inventor Cornelis Drebbel.

Underground trains

Let's set the scene . . . you're in 19th-century London, the Industrial Revolution is happening and the population is growing FAST. A new transport idea was needed, and in 1863, the first ever underground railway opened: the Metropolitan Railway. Today, over 190 cities have a similar network.

SHARKS OR MOUNT EVEREST?

Surely the enormous, rocky Mount Everest – the highest mountain in the WHOLE WORLD – came first? It did not! There were sharks in our seas long before Everest formed – and before the dinosaurs appeared, too.

Sharks

The ancestors of sharks were alive about 420 million years ago. At this point, Earth had just two big continents: Laurussia in the north and Gondwana in the south. Over time, these continents changed in shape and size as they moved around the globe, eventually forming the continents you'd recognise today.

Mount Everest

Around 50 million years ago, the continents of Earth were (very slowly) on the move. The land masses that make up India and the rest of Asia today bumped into each other. The land that became crunched up where they met, gradually formed the Himalaya mountain range, where Mount Everest stands.

Everest is still growing – around 4 millimetres each year!

Incredible fossils

Some rocks and fossils found near the summit of Everest are from sea creatures and plants. Before India and Asia collided, the sands and muds that would later form the rocks of the Himalayas were underwater. As they rose up, the remains of animals and plants were lifted with them.

FLYING AROUND THE WORLD OR DIVING TO THE BOTTOM OF THE SEA?

If you said flying, good guess – you're correct. Strap in for extreme adventures!

Flying

On 6 April 1924, four American military planes set off from Seattle in north-western USA. Their mission was to fly around the world, stopping off only for refuelling and repairs. All the crew members survived, and they landed back in Seattle on 28 September 1924, after nearly six months of travel. Hurrah!

Diving

The very deepest part of the ocean is the Mariana Trench, in the Pacific ocean. Getting there is a tricky job. Deep water creates a huge amount of pressure, more than humans can survive in, so specially-designed vehicles are needed for deep-sea travel. The first dive to reach the bottom of the sea was in 1960, 36 years after the US military flight around the world.

The ocean isn't the same depth everywhere – there are mountain ranges, valleys and shallow plains, just like on land.

TREES OR THE SAHARA DESERT?

Trees. The first trees evolved almost 400 million years ago – scientists estimate that the Sahara became a desert around 5–2 million years ago. It has had different climates over time and has been home to lakes, plants and forests!

HUMANS OR SPACE ROVERS WALKING ON THE MOON?

Space rovers are remote-controlled robots that can move around far away from the scientists controlling them. They are incredibly useful for exploration of the Moon, but it was people who walked there first!

Humans on the Moon

On 20 July 1969, as part of the USA's Apollo 11 mission, astronauts Neil Armstrong and Buzz Aldrin became the first two people to step onto the Moon's surface. As Armstrong left the rocket, he spoke the famous words, "That's one small step for [a] man, one giant leap for mankind."

Rovers on the Moon

The first fully mobile, remote-controlled lunar rover wasn't far behind people. Lunokhod 1, a Soviet rover, landed on 17 November 1970. It travelled around 10.5 kilometres, exploring and analysing samples of soil. It sent over 20,000 images of the Moon back to Earth!

Ready . . . set . . . ROCKETS!

The missions to the Moon were part of the Space Race between the USA and the Soviet Union, who both wanted to be the best at space travel. It was a close race. In February 1969, five months before the USA's Apollo 11 mission, the Soviet Union tried to launch a rover to the Moon, but it failed to get out of Earth's atmosphere.

Astro-golf!
Astronaut Alan Shepard hit a golf ball on the Moon during his spacewalk in 1971!

Though rovers reached the Moon after astronauts, some spacecraft did land before humans got there. These pieces of equipment took photographs and gathered data – but they couldn't move around by themselves!

SATURN'S RINGS OR EARTH?

You might be surprised to find out that Saturn and its rings are not the same age! Earth and Saturn are both much older.

Earth
Our planet formed around 4.6 billion years ago, when gravity pulled particles of gas and dust together. The other planets in our Solar System formed around the same time – Saturn's iconic rings, though, came much later . . .

Saturn's rings
Many space scientists think that the rings, which are made from chunks of ice and rocky dust, were formed around 100 million years ago. It's still not completely clear how this happened, but some scientists think the rings were created when a couple of Saturn's moons bumped into each other and shattered.

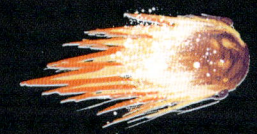

Stegosaurus, sharks and many other animals and dinosaurs are all older than Saturn's rings, too.

In 2020, NASA delivered an updated space toilet to the International Space Station. It allowed waste liquid to be collected and recycled into drinking water on the space station!

SPACE RADIOS OR SPACE TOILETS?

It was space radios – but not for music!

Radios
When astronauts take off to fly many kilometres above the Earth, a team of scientists stay behind and track their progress. Regular updates are important! Yuri Gagarin, the first human to go into space in 1961, used a communication system based on radio waves.

Toilets
The first astronauts to go into space didn't have toilets at all. They wore nappies under their space suits, or collected the waste in bags! It wasn't until 1973 that the first space toilet was created. Astronauts had to poo into a hole in the wall – it was then dried out with a fan.

FOOTBALL MATCHES OR RUNNING RACES?

Ready . . . set . . . RUN! People were racing each other on foot long before football was created.

Running races

Humans have been running for millions of years, so it's impossible to say when the first running race was. There were some famous ancient events though . . . such as the Olympics! This iconic competition started in 776BCE, in ancient Greece. At the first one (and perhaps others) there was one event: a running race. This race, called the *stadion*, was around 192 metres long – just under the length of two football pitches. Speaking of which . . .

Football matches

Games where a ball is kicked (or kicked and thrown) between players have been around for over 2,000 years – but football as we know it today was created as recently as the 1800s. Why the big time gap? Let's find out . . .

Football through time

Throughout football's history, there have been LOTS of small differences in rules between teams. During the 1800s, teams began using improved road and train networks to play teams further afield. A standard set of rules was needed for everyone to follow – in 1863, the world's first Football Association formed in London and created the Laws of the Game. Phew! Today, the International Football Association Board is responsible for the Laws.

The ancient Greeks played a ball game called Episkyros, which was a bit like American football. In the ancient Chinese ball game Cuju, the ball wasn't allowed to touch the ground.

WINTER OLYMPIC GAMES OR PARALYMPIC GAMES?

Better wrap up warm – it was the Winter Olympics that came first. Let's head into the mountains of France to find out more . . .

Winter Olympic Games

The first Winter Olympics were held in Chamonix, in the French Alps, in 1924. The snowy events included figure skating, ski jumping, bobsleigh and ice hockey. In 1976, the first Winter Paralympic Games took place in Örnsköldsvik, Sweden.

The first Paralympics took place in Rome in 1960 and included around 400 athletes. At the Paris Paralympic Games in 2024, there were around 4,400 athletes!

Paralympic Games

German doctor Ludwig Guttman was central to the start of the Paralympics. He worked at Stoke Mandeville Hospital in England, treating World War II veterans with paraplegia (paralysis in the lower body). He organised sporting competitions called the Stoke Mandeville Games from 1948 to help with their recovery and coincide with the Olympics. Archery was the only event in the first games, but more were gradually added. The games eventually became known as the Paralympic Games in 1960.

AZTECS OR VIKINGS?

Is that the sound of clashing swords and splashing oars . . . yes, it was the Vikings! The Viking Age began around 1,200 years ago. The Aztec empire, on the other hand, started around 700 years ago.

Vikings
The Viking Age began when Scandinavians left northern Europe in the 8th century CE to look for wealth. One of the first Viking raids was around 793CE, to England's north-east island of Lindisfarne, but they travelled much further, including to North America.

Settling starts
The last Viking invasion in England was in 1066CE, over 950 years ago. Scandinavians were no longer just raiders – many had settled as farmers and traders.

Aztecs
The Aztec empire began in 1325, in the city of Tenochtitlan, in the area we now know as Mexico. The Aztecs created their own religion, rulers and farming systems, but in 1521, their civilisation was defeated after an invasion by Spanish soldiers known as conquistadors.

ANCIENT ROME OR ANCIENT EGYPT?

Mummies, pyramids, pharaohs . . . yes, it was the ancient Egyptians!

Ancient Egypt
The ancient Egyptian Kingdom began a whopping 5,000 years ago – that's around 2,000 years before ancient Rome! The two did overlap though. When ancient Egyptian queen Cleopatra lost a battle with the future Roman emperor Augustus, Egypt became part of the Roman empire.

Ancient Rome
The ancient Roman empire started with the city of Rome, but its foundation is a mystery. Most of our knowledge comes from stories and myths. The date most historians give for Rome's foundation is 753 BCE but people probably lived in the area a few centuries earlier, around 3,000 years ago.

THE GREAT PYRAMID OF GIZA OR THE GREEK PARTHENON?

The Great Pyramid! It was completed around 2500 BCE, as a tomb for the ancient Egyptian pharaoh Khufu. The Parthenon was built in Athens between 447–432 BCE, as a temple dedicated to the goddess of Athena – whom the city was named after!

TIMELINE

You've finished all the questions, hooray! How many did you guess correctly?

Explore this timeline to see some of the amazing events and discoveries covered in this book. The early years are approximate.

1620 First submarine dive

1810 First tin cans

1858 First can opener

1863 First underground railway opens

1903 First plane flight

1907 First helicopter flight

1913 Electric fridge invented

1583 First theme park

1391 First toilet paper created

1325 Aztec empire begins

793 CE Vikings first raid England

600 CE Chaturanga (chess ancestor) invented

105 CE Paper invented

420 million years ago First sharks

400 million years ago First trees

155–150 million years ago Stegosaurus lived

68–66 million years ago Tyrannosaurus lived

50 million years ago Mount Everest formed

1924 First plane flight around the world

1945 Microwave oven invented

1958 First video game

1960 First Mariana Trench dive

1965 First skate park opened Touch screen invented

1975 First portable digital camera

1999 First emojis created

200 BCE First game of rock, paper, scissors

447–432 BCE The Parthenon is built

753 BCE Ancient Rome founded

1400 BCE Alquerque (draughts ancestor) invented

1500 BCE Minoan flushing toilet built

2000 BCE Woolly mammoths become extinct

*BCE means Before the Common Era (the birth of Jesus Christ). CE means after the Common Era.

5–2 million years ago The Sahara becomes a desert

1.5 million years ago First blue whales

8000 BCE* First boats

3500 BCE First wheels

3100 BCE Ancient Egyptian Kingdom begins

2500 BCE The Great Pyramid of Giza is completed